Alligator, Owl, Rabbit, Friends and The Snake

SHERRY BLAKENEY

To order additional copies of this book, contact:
Xlibris LLC
1-888-795-4274
www.Xlibris.com
Orders@Xlibris.com

Alligator, Owl, Rabbit, Friends and The Snake

There were three friends with powerful thinking abilities, Tajon the alligator who is an engineer, Cortney an owl who is a doctor and Ashley the rabbit who is an attorney. All brilliant in their careers, they each brought beautiful homes worth millions, the doctor served the LORD in her home, giving and helping the homeless and others, in her deeds, the doctor was always under the influence of Jesus, beautiful, stunning and respected among all for her quick wittiness in medicine. Her friend the alligator held GREAT FAITH he believed that God could do anything, caring with his compassion to love people and help the less educated, he also served the LORD, his bright brilliant intellect and dress attire was envied by another engineers and the last person among the circle was an attorney she was prefect in her beauty, long curly silky hair, a face of a queen, soft, sweet, most radiant, stunning, ravishing attorney with all grace, envied by all because of her beauty and cleverness, keen decision making, brilliant in making things happen. She served the LORD with joy in her heart and love in her hands. They were all among people of great power "THE ELITE" greed and prejudice against people of less financial status; words of hate filled the hearts of the pride and greed. But the Alligator, Owl and Rabbit hearts were always filled with compassion and love for all people.

SHERRY BLAKENEY

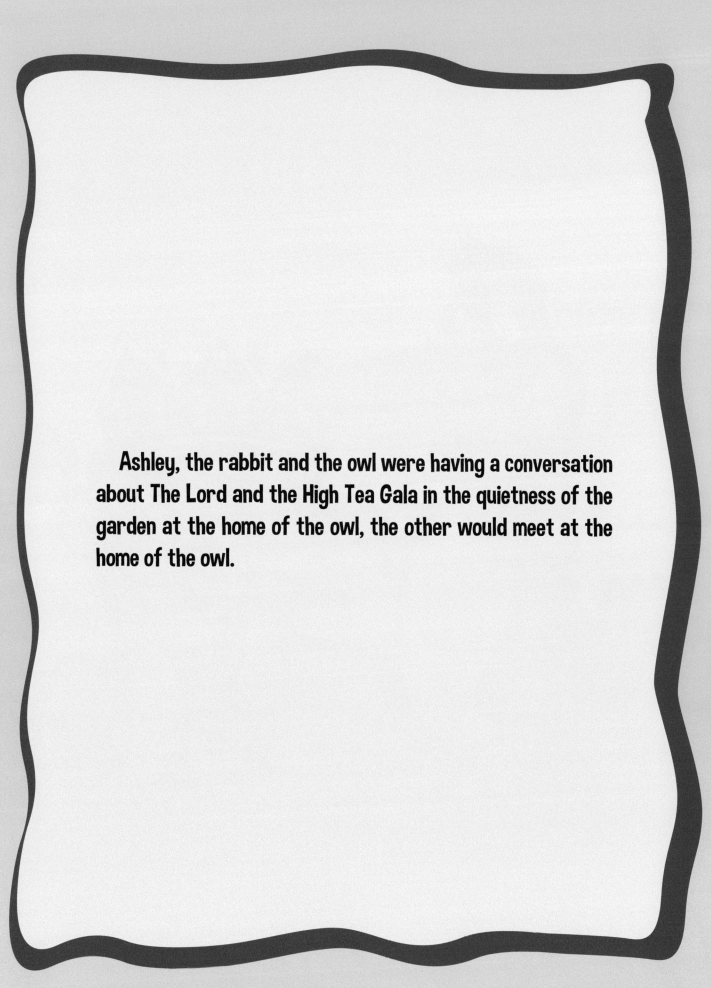

Ashley, the rabbit and the owl were having a conversation about The Lord and the High Tea Gala in the quietness of the garden at the home of the owl, the other would meet at the home of the owl.

Alligator was headed to the owl's home to join in the conversation with his friends but suddenly, John, the snake walked up and tried to convince alligator he would profit more if he would disconnect with The Lord and his friends, he explained to him that he didn't need them, but the alligator did not want to hear a word from the month of the snake. So, alligator continued on to the home of owl.

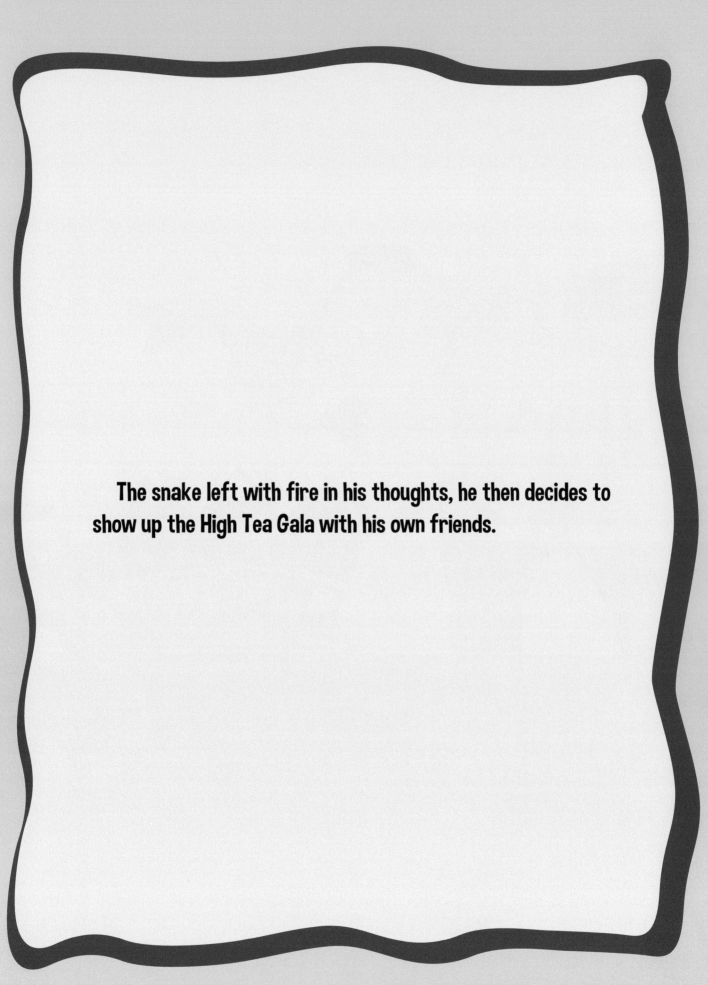

The snake left with fire in his thoughts, he then decides to show up the High Tea Gala with his own friends.

Will, the elephant was a friend of the owl, he was traveling a long way to owl's home and on his way, he run into the snake, snake again tried to convince another to joint his circle of friends and disconnect with The Lord, but the elephant spoke with GREAT POWER in his voice and said NO!, the elephant continued to travel to owl's home.

While at home, Daniel, the Lion was delighted to know he would attend this big event, daydreaming about how he would be of help to the owl and rabbit to help the homeless, they had raised thousands of dollars to denote funds for the building of homes for the homeless, and then came a **LOUD KNOCK** at the door, it was the snake trying and trying again to bring someone in his circle but, the Lion **ROARED IN THE STRENGTH OF POWER** and said No! And closed the door of this fancy home, on the face of the snake, He walked away in **GREAT** disappointment.

The race of the James, the Jaguar and Javon, the cheetah would soon be over and the cheetah won the race, soon after the race the snake introduced his self to the cheetah and asked him to become part of his circle because he only wanted the best, but, there would be conditions with the friendship, the cheetah ran **FAST** and spoke the words of **CERTAINLY NOT**, the snake fire was being put out.

Brittany, the Liger was at home studying her medical book on a patient problem, before going over the home of the owl, **SUDDENLY**, a cry for help was at her door the snake said to the liger would you help me but, the tiger was never liked snakes; get away from my home, she **ROARED** with great power of 10th ligers and the snake ran as fast as he could away from the liger.

Leah, the fox was at home looking at her fancy dresses to wear to the home of the owl, when the snake appeared in her room, the fox said where did you come from, you must go **NOW**, but the snake tried to speak to the fox and she picked him up and throw him out of her home, the snake said no more, I will see them all at the High Tea Gala!

The friends of the owl's, soon all arrived at the home of the owl to discuss the plans of The Lord's work and all would give to the building of the homes for the homeless.

The circle of the Pride and Greed would try to stop the compassion of the owl's plan, but the Lord wouldn't have it. So, the storm came up.

The night started off as a clear night, the three friends attended a cocktail party with all the elite of social society, and there was laughter, strategizing conversations, pride and greed that filled the atmosphere. As the night went along, there was dancing and drinking of sparkling apple cider, it all seem delightful with the high society, the cocktail party ended just a little after midnight, outside the clouds grew, the sky became dark, within a short time the rain started, with great thunder, this storm would take down homes of pride and greed, the storm was powerful, the winds were gusting with incredible winds, the lightening was speaking with a ROAR, the rain poured down like an UNSTOPPABLE SEA.

The three friends arrived at home safely, as the wind roared the lightning increased the greed starting praying that the storm would end and all would be well, but the winds increased and fear THUMP in the heart of the pride and greed, all of the homes of the pride would come down during the storm, winds of GREAT STRENGTH and POWERFUL RAIN brought down the homes, many lessons would be learned on that day, the alligator, owl and rabbit were safe from the storm, without a scratch of damage to their homes, large trees fell on the homes of the pride and many people were without home. Love never fails. Love never gives up.

THE END

Printed in the United States
by Baker & Taylor Publisher Services